Dear Student:

Inside the Twisted Mind of an Exasperated Professor

Also By Ilana S. Lehmann, Ph.D.

All You Need to Know About Disability is on Star Trek

The Completely Useless Dictionary of Higher Education

Dear Student:

Inside the Twisted Mind of an Exasperated Professor

by Ilana S. Lehmann, Ph.D.

Mind Meld Media

Dear Student: Inside the Twisted Mind of an Exasperated Professor. Copyright 2015 by Mind Meld Media, LLC. All rights reserved. Printed in the United States of America. No part of this book may be used or reproduced in any manner whatsoever without the written permission of the publisher. Mind Meld Media, is a Limited Liability Corporation in the state of Delaware with its principal offices at 5313 NE 66th Ave G55, Vancouver, WA 98661.

Edited by Susan Frager
Cover design by Jay Arnold at www.thelogonom.com
Proofreading by Donald R. Janousek

Library of Congress Control Number: 2015900596

Lehmann, Ilana S., 1961 -
 Dear Student: Inside the Twisted Mind of an
 Exasperated Professor   / Ilana S. Lehmann
 p. cm
 ISBN 978-0-9904540-2-1

All rights reserved.
Printed in the United States of America.

To all my former students who read the syllabus, wrote beautifully in their own words, and only emailed me in professional tones—thanks for nothing.

Preface

Twitter is like a nightclub where a comedian can try out their material to see what is truly funny. I created "Dear Student" tweets to vent my frustration while making other people laugh at the absurdity of the poor writing I was grading. By turning my frustrations into humor, grading became less of a chore and more of an opportunity to explore my own twisted mind. I consider retweets and favorites to be endorsements. Nothing I tweet is made up. It isn't necessary. My students provide me with an ample supply of material. Everything within quotation marks has appeared in a student's paper.

Not all of my students write as if they're illiterate. Good writers make up the majority of my classes. Alas, good writers are rarely as funny. At the same time, I have been amazed that so many graduate school students cannot write a grammatically correct sentence. Twitter is not for everyone, so I've de-hashtagged the "Dear Student" tweets so everyone can enjoy the fun.

Chapter 1: Student Types

Braggers

Dear Student,

Did you think I would be so impressed by your self-proclaimed career as a writer that I wouldn't notice the five typos in your introduction?

You couldn't have possibly have written "Last, but definitely not least . . . ." This is a research paper, not your acceptance speech.

I'm not impressed by your Ivy League undergraduate degree. You must impress me with what you do in my class.

Please don't write in your class introduction that you're a "people person." I find you annoying already.

Why do I need to know your father is an attorney? Are you planning to do something dishonest?

I see you take pride in your non-conformity. You should be thrilled with your out-of-the-mainstream grade.

Debaters

Dear Student,

You're in graduate school but you don't have an MS degree yet. I have a PhD. Explain again how you *know* you are right.

Telling me other professors think your writing is good is not a persuasive argument. Based on this paper, it is not even believable.

Cheaters

Dear Student,

I'm not giving you credit for seventeen pages when you only wrote nine. Spacing is like air and your paper was full of air. (And error)

Why would you want a master's degree based on plagiarism? You will know you're a fraud, even if you don't get caught.

Yes, I'm asking questions so you dig yourself in deeper. You've already been caught using someone else's paper. Shovel?

Please tell me again how you wrote this paper at another university when your transcripts show you never went there.

Your explanation that you worked with someone else on this paper doesn't make sense. Your paper matched one written eight years ago. That's working ahead!

Please explain how your paper was 90% similar to a paper submitted to another college. I hope you can get your money back.

According to the document properties you spent 47 minutes on two drafts of this paper. You said you spent "days." Explains much.

Gamers

Dear Student,

I just love it when you add eight lines of spacing at the bottom of each page. It makes your grade a total surprise. Surprise!

I see what you did there. Putting the conclusion on a separate page will not fool me into thinking you have more pages.

You wrote twice as much as required. Unfortunately, 80% was fluff.

Congratulations on saying the same thing in four sentences using slightly different words. Still only counts as one answer.

Yours is not the first student paper that has tried to masquerade as meeting page number requirements with "creative spacing."

Once you can fake sincerity, compassion, and honesty, you are well on your way to becoming a good criminal.

Word Count Strivers

At times, assignments have word count minimums to indicate to the student how much depth is expected in their papers. The requirement results in mixed outcomes. When I see feeble attempts at meeting the word count requirements, I worry that my students think I am so old, that I don't see through their shenanigans.

Dear Student,

When you say "disasters" you don't need to list them. I have been teaching a long time. I know all about disasters.

Please tell me the differences among "emergencies, disasters and catastrophes" (other than word count.)

Your use of article titles in addition to the authors' names spoke volumes to me about your word count fears.

The word is *everyone*. "…for communities, environment, elderly, disable, children and many groups in society."

You used "et al." in your last paper, so I know you're repeating the names of all five authors multiple times in this paper to increase your word count.

I know there's a minimum page count. I know you've run out of things to say. But repeatedly using an author's first name is really bad fluff.

"…are defined more so than ever before in past decades" Ah yes, I see you're trying to meet that minimum word count.

"In the technological age that we find ourselves living in within the United States of America," Worried about word count?

When you copy and paste the instructions into your post, you're not increasing your word count.

Your paper has so much filler, it makes a hotdog look wholesome.

Slackers

Dear Student,

Nothing says "Hard Working Student" like having the same format errors on your references page in every assignment. Do you ever read my comments?

I promise to take as much diligence finding you every point possible, as you did completing this assignment.

There's a big difference between a lack of research and your inability to find the research. Have you ever heard of librarians?

I'm sorry other professors have not been as hard on you as I am. That's why you haven't learned what you need to know.

The 180 words you quoted isn't counted in the 200 word minimum. I know your type. That's why the syllabus says "original work."

Expecting an A just because you turned in a paper, is like expecting weight loss because you bought exercise equipment. You must do the work.

My surprise was that you didn't correct the errors I identified when I allowed you to rewrite your paper. Your surprise will be your grade.

You may have to work harder in my class than others. Just think how happy you'll be when you get through it. Me too.

Even though hard work has never yet killed a student, I see you're not taking any chances.

Entitled

Dear Student,

Let's review: You failed the paper because of plagiarism. Your grade appeal failed. Now you want me to grant you a rewrite? I'll give you this, you've got chutzpah!

Of course it's the library's fault your references weren't from peer-reviewed sources. It's not like *you* picked them out, right?

I know you think I'm a lousy instructor because you don't understand the materials. Do you have any idea what I think of you?

I have a sensitive "entitlement" warning system. You have just set it off. Loudly.

Thanks for calling me on a Saturday to ask about the email you sent three minutes ago. I was only doing laundry, and other life stuff. Nothing important.

I see your "entitlement attitude" and raise you one case of "you didn't follow the instructions." I win.

Third time you've asked when I'm available for a meeting. You've never set anything up. Do you just want to keep track of me?

The directions are clear. My guess is you don't want to read them because they're long. No, I am not going to summarize them for you.

Yes, you *can* get a C in this course. You earned it. I guess you won't be getting reimbursed by your employer. So sad.

Whiners

Dear Student,

This is an online course. I don't know you well enough to like or dislike you. I can't be responsible for your assumptions.

Thank you for complaining about how I'm *picky* about your spelling and grammar. This is a writing course, that's my job!

Feel free to send me emails complaining about emails I didn't answer. It's hard to answer emails I didn't receive. Try spelling my name right next time.

If you want to hear how wonderful you are, send your paper to your mom. If you want to learn how to improve, listen to me.

It's hard to feel sorry for someone who has three instructors to please when I have over sixty-five students who want a piece of me.

Of course I won't make you follow the rules now that you have told me how much you hate them. -Said no professor, ever.

Chapter 2: Welcome to the Virtual Class

Love the Internet

Dear Student,

Why in the name of Vulcan logic would you sign up for an online course if you have "unreliable" Internet? No extension. Bam!

You missed the paper because your job training came unexpectedly? Just you're your employer provide documentation of the *surprise* training.

Why did you *guess* what fire gear weighs? You're taking an online course. That means you could look it up on the Internet. Oh, and you're a bad guesser.

If you don't want to listen to the lectures; don't be surprised by the grade you earn. I didn't record those lectures for me.

Discussion Board Posts

Teaching in online courses usually involves students posting on a discussion board, with other students being required to comment on their posts. The topics are called threads. Within a thread, there will be one or more questions. Minimum word counts provide a guideline about the depth of analysis expected from the assigned readings. The idea is to build a learning community. The result is not always so scholarly.

Dear Student,

When you begin a post "First and foremost," two things come to mind. First: cliché. And foremost: word count.

Thanks for the email. So you think your 47 word discussion board response should get the same grade as the student who wrote 217 words?

If you hadn't missed answering the third question, you wouldn't have needed the fluff or been short on the word count.

When you post using outside sources I don't think, "Wow, this student did extra work." I assume you didn't read the book.

When you begin a post with "To be completely honest" I start to wonder about the veracity of your other posts.

You posted a request for a rewrite in on the discussion board. And I deleted it. You got your answer. Next question?

Pro Tip: Avoid multiple clichés such as "wet behind the ears," "thrown to the wolves," and "down the road" in the same post!

If you want to impress me when you respond to a fellow student, start an argument. Not everything posted is wonderful.

Your discussion post reminded me of an old John Wayne western. Instead of *shooting from the hip*, try citing sources.

Your posts sound like a horoscope prediction. Vague enough to apply to anything, based on the stars, and not a credible source.

The question was "What surprised you about the study?" Posting that you were surprised misses the point. Surprise!

Posts are Graded

Dear Student,

Posting long quotations from the book is not the same thing as *writing* a post. How do I grade the book?

Even after I posted that I was aware of this website you cut and pasted from it? I can't decide if you are being unethical or just dumb.

Nothing quite says "I don't care" like a 50 word post when there is a 200 word minimum.

Your post was interesting, probably more interesting than answers to the discussion questions. Too bad they weren't related.

Re-using a discussion post from the beginning of the term only works if the instructor is senile.

Posts are dated. You don't get credit for late posts. They don't count. Don't bother. No points. Stop it already. Go away.

Communication

Dear Student,

Thanks for the post, text, and voicemail letting me know you sent me an email. I just love that feeling of being stalked.

You had no discussion posts. You submitted four out of ten assignments. All four were submitted late. Please tell me why you're surprised you failed.

Don't call a professor without an appointment. Did you really expect me to answer? During dinner?

Just because I am grading at the crack of dawn on a Sunday, doesn't mean you can call me at the crack of dawn on Sunday.

Email is not the only means of communication. It's not even the most efficient.

You've Got to be Kidding Me

Dear Student,

You didn't know quotations needed quotation marks? Didn't you ever wonder how those little marks got their name?

Don't worry now about your missing paper; I've already submitted your grade. I hope that your vacation was worth it.

Sorry I disturbed your beach vacation with my silly request for you to edit your assignment to meet the requirements.

When you respond to your fellow classmate's post, keep in mind that "Way to go!" is more a greeting than a response.

This online course has a thing called tracking. I know where you've been and for how long. It's not stalking per se . . .

Please tell me how *celebrating* Columbus Day prevented you from writing the paper. It's not exactly a big holiday . . . .

Only two weeks of class left. Not a good time to ask for an extension. Sorry about your vacation plans.

There is a difference between writing in social media and writing a research paper! No smiley faces, ever!

Of course you can miss the last three weeks of the semester. No problem. Unless you want to pass the course . . . .

Chapter 3: From Me to You

Advice

Dear Student,

If you're going to be a smartass, first you have to be smart. Otherwise, you're just an ass.

If you are looking for a professor with the patience of a saint, maybe you should try divinity school.

Don't try to impress me with your vocabulary. Impress me with the depth of your understanding. Complex ideas in simple words.

An assumption on your part does not constitute a reality on my part.

If you're trying to impress me by citing one of my publications, you should be careful to spell my name correctly.

"Yes" is not an answer to a question that begins with "Why."

When your professor tells you she lives on the West Coast, take that as a hint not to request an East Coast early morning appointment time.

If you are going to take the time to discuss the book of a famous author, be sure you use the correct pronoun in your presentation.

When trying to kiss up to the professor I strongly suggest you make a greater effort to spell my name correctly.

Thanks for the suggestion, but I won't be making the final project a group assignment. Too many redshirts in the classes.

When the question is "What surprised you about . . . ?" Your response should include the word "surprised".

No, getting married during the term will not excuse you from due dates. Maybe you should take a leave of absence.

"Did attempt" = "attempted". Is this the best you can do to meet the word count requirements?

Comparisons

Dear Student,

Your argument makes about as much sense as a knitted condom and is just as useful.

Corresponding with you over email feels like I am being stoned to death with popcorn.

Environments can't make people act a certain way. Otherwise, being in graduate school would *make* you use follow the style manual and it doesn't.

You are as demanding as my cat, but a hell of a lot easier to ignore.

I don't give grades; students earn them. I am not Santa Claus; I am your employer.

Creating larger committees rarely improves outcomes. An elephant is probably a mouse created by a large committee.

Don't cite sources not listed on your references list, and don't reference sources you don't cite. It's like matching socks!

Reading your twelve-page paper without headings, was like trying to drive in a new city where no one put up road signs. I'm lost.

Having a reference you didn't cite, is like putting a philosophy book on your bookshelf so others will think you're smart.

Grading your paper reminded me of a scavenger hunt. I knew what I was looking for, but had to look in several places to find it.

Asking a professor about Christmas plans before learning if the professor celebrates it–is like buying a textbook without knowing which one is assigned.

Would you buy bathroom scales that compute how hard you *tried* to stick to your diet when it gives your weight? Okay, let's try another example . . .

You have required more patience than training my cat. And you are equally compliant.

You used a free essays website. I used the plagiarism checker. It's like the Spy vs. Spy from Mad Magazine all over again!

Submitting the same paper to two different courses is like trying to pay for item X with the same $5 you used to buy item Y.

It is not enough just to parrot back the information. Unless, of course, you are a parrot.

That's Just Rude

Dear Student,

Before class, turn off your cell phone ringer. If you do not know how to turn off the ringer, then you're too stupid to own a cell phone much less be in a PhD program.

Sunday night I agreed to meet on Monday. I waited all day. Good morning, today is Tuesday. You better be dead.

When texting your professor before the sun is up, do not use "LOL" in the message. It's too early for anyone to be laughing.

My first name is *doctor*, why do you ask? Initials are there for a reason.

Sorry your undergraduate program never taught you how to address a professor. Here's a hint–"Hey" is not a good start.

Asking for a letter of recommendation between semesters is not good timing. Give me my break.

When I point out you didn't follow the directions; you don't endear yourself by calling me "nitpicky".

Warnings

Dear Student,

When you stand up your professor for the third time, I hope you know that bad things will happen.

Life is full of choices. You chose graduate school. This means you're temporarily giving up having a life.

Lack of planning on your part, does not constitute an emergency on my part.

Chapter 4: Words

At times, I have to remind myself that my students have already completed an undergraduate degree by the time they enroll in my courses. The poor spelling, grammar, and lack of proofreading can be highly frustrating. This chapter contains some of my "pet peeves."

And

Dear Student,

" . . . this research is to search and discover similarities and differences in the criminal activities and behavior . . . " Too much "and."

I'm playing a game with your paper. I am trying to find a single sentence without the word "and." Wish me luck!

I hate your writing instructor! "Accurate and exact data . . . ." Tell me why you need both of these words.

You are hereby limited to only one "and" per sentence. Don't make me put you on a comma diet too!

Did some evil English teacher tell you that every sentence should have an "and" in it?

Very

Dear Student,

If you used your paper for a drinking game (take a shot for every *very*) it would probably kill you. It killed me.

I could fail you just based on the fact you wrote *very* fifteen times in your paper.

What are the differences between *very different* and *different*? Yeah, I could not think of one either.

Congratulations on your use of the word *imperative*. That is so much better than "very, very important."

I think if I read one more "very important" . . . I will need a padded room!

You have used "very" nine times:
- "very important" (four times),
- "very serious" (twice),
- "very key,"
- "very great," and
- "very vital."

I'm very sad.

Really? You were "very extremely surprised" by the finding? I could only muster a *facepalm* when I read that sentence.

I have forbidden the use of "very" in research papers. Don't make me add "it" to the list! Research is specific. It isn't.

If you want to use "very" in your research paper you will need an executive order from the President and an act of Congress.

Wordiness

Dear Student,

"Time and time again…" One word: Repeatedly.

If you write "system" three times in one sentence, you probably need to re-write the sentence.

Saying the same thing repeatedly for ten pages is not a research proposal. How can I describe it? Death by wordiness.

Just as I was becoming less annoyed by students writing in word pairs, you wrote in word trios. Now I am annoyed, pissed off, and riled.

I need a separate rubric to grade your work. This one only covers research papers, not verbal diarrhea.

This isn't public speaking, it's a research paper. You don't need to tell me what you already told me. *Facepalm.*

Too many words! "The belief here is that this is the way..."

Why are you putting *do* in front of verbs? There's no difference between "do try" and "tries" or "did attempt" and "attempted." Just ask Yoda.

Wrong word

Dear Student,

There are funny differences between "illicit responses" and "elicit responses." So funny, I can't stop laughing.

"Since the 1960s the structure of family has experienced intense progressions." I had no idea progressions could be intense.

Interesting choice of adjective, "ferocious behavior of children." I have never heard children referred to as *tigers* before . . . .

"In my research I would use *ground* theory." I guess that is a hard and cold theory?

"The scared tactics that were utilized . . ." So what were the tactics afraid of, other than your poor grammar?

"Extensive studies being conducted on weather justice is more beneficial . . . " Raining justice? The word is "whether".

So are those "clear rolls" a type of transparent pastry? I wish I had thought of that, but it wasn't my role.

You don't mean "pin pointed" unless the pin was doing the pointing. Pinpoint is only one word.

When you wrote "by in large" you meant "by and large". Let me guess, you can tell me a lot about podcasts because you know nothing of grammar.

"Inappropriate" is over-used. Picking your nose in public is bad manners. Masturbating in public is disgusting behavior.

You meant "abnormal" not "paranormal." They aren't the same thing.

You mean throughout the "world," not the "globe." A globe is like a three-D map. Were you watching a Harry Potter movie last night?

A person should "pass muster" not "pass mustard" . . . unless they are at a picnic.

Until I read your paper, I haven't noticed how "violent" and "violet" look a lot alike. Trying to picture "violet behavior."

One does not "spout off" unless one is a whale.

A coma is a medical condition; a comma is a punctuation mark.

"More agitating is the fact . . . " You mean "aggravating." Your paper is agitating, your statistic is aggravating.

When you wrote "due to grater violence," did you mean cheese graters are being used as weapons?

Did you really just write we need "stiffer registration requirements for sex offenders"? Stiffer? Really?

Unless you are writing about scatology, the word poop should not be used in your paper. By the way, it is also not an adjective.

"In other words and in theory" are not the same thing. What the %$#% do you mean?

When talking about three systems don't conclude using the word "it" because I can't be certain which one you're referring to.

We *comb* hair; we *search* for journal articles. Yes. I know it's confusing.

When you wrote "The Black community is pledged with crime . . . " The word you wanted was *plagued*.

The word is "said". As in, "she said." She did not "go like!"

A "literature review" is not the same as a "literary review".

Thanks for the laughs. You meant "parenthetical citations". You wrote "pathetic citations". In your case, there wasn't a lot of difference.

There are big differences between "less children" and "childrenless".

The researchers aspired, sought, undertook, attempted, examined, studied . . . but they didn't *hope* to find. Trust me, researchers have little hope.

You can't have people from European America. It is not a place. People can be European Americans. That's different.

Articles are *cited* not *sighted*. Look! Over there. It's a research article.

"I must omit this course was challenging to myself" Honestly said, and self-evident.

The term you were trying to write was *re-incarceration* not *reincarnation*. These words are worlds apart.

The study used children, not kids. Kids are baby goats. Baby goats aren't allowed in school because they chew up books.

Cite, site, and sight are *not* the same. When in doubt, look it up!

If the researcher collected "every day" the researcher is collecting daily. If the researcher collected "everyday" things, the research collected common items.

When someone has children, do not refer to the event as "he knocked-up his girlfriend" in a graduate school paper.

There and their; they're not the same!

Writing a sentence with a double negative is a no-no.

When you are tempted to write "and/or" pick one, "And" means "both"; "or" means "one of these". You can't mean "both" and "one."

If it's 'exactly the same' that means it's identical. If it's 'almost the same' that means it's not the same, but similar. So, what does "almost exactly the same" mean?

Yes, it was just as you said, "As peviously stated . . . " I can't stop laughing.

I am glad you have so many big words in your vocabulary. The next step is to learn how to use them correctly.

Chapter 5: Writing

Examples of Bad Writing

Dear Student,

"Impasses of meaning was discovered" Obviously your goal is to avoid making sense, and you're doing a bang-up job of it!

"Pending comparatively currently, the central point of research, policy and involvement." Are you intentionally trying to kill my brain cells?

"*Ethics* and *morality* are theoretical frameworks which weigh heavily in the pursuit of justice." I would like to see your scale.

It doesn't get much more passive voice than this! "An importance lies within proper communication."

Writing

Dear Student,

Please, for the sake of my brain cells . . . will you come to the point?

Did you put your entire vocabulary in that sentence?

The reason you're told not to write in passive voice is that it has a tendency to put the reader to sleep. Zzzzzz

Given the number of mistakes in this paper, please assure me that you will never attempt to work with subatomic particles or heavy machinery.

There are so many errors in this project, I feel like a mosquito in a nudist colony. I don't know where to start.

In the words of Monty Python: "Your mother was a hamster and your father smelt of elderberries!" Plus your writing stinks!

Thanks for letting me read the rough draft of your assignment. Don't bother sending me the final version. I graded this one.

I'm going to assume that this is your first term in graduate school and in the US. Otherwise I'll need to cry myself to sleep tonight.

If someone breaks into your house and steals your thesaurus, could you still write like this? Not that I would do that.

Your need to improve on summarizing and paraphrasing isn't "something to keep in mind for next time." It's required this time.

After having graded three of your papers, I am glad you are getting out of your current career. Lawyers should be able to write.

Comma Abuse

Dear Student,

You had, so many, commas, in your intro,— I could hear Captain Kirk's voice while reading it.

"Research is not cut and, dry it is a difficult process" - And apparently, so is your punctuation.

Punctuation Missing in Action

Dear Student,

Have you ever heard of commas? They're not just used in citations. They make long sentences readable—and they're free!

Commas are not ending punctuation marks—except in your paper.

All sentences should end with a punctuation mark. There are several models to choose from.

The only thing worse than too many commas is no commas. Commas are helpful, and they're cute. They look like tadpoles.

Quotation Marks

Dear Student,

Please use quotation marks when quoting. They are available at no cost and can be found above the apostrophe key.

I had a choice of seeing the missing quotation marks as plagiarism or format errors–which only reduced your grade. Did I choose the wrong one?

Keep calm and don't use exclamation marks in a research paper.

Begin and end quotes with quotation marks. That way I won't assume the rest of this paper is all part of the first quote.

A research question is not the same thing as a hypothesis. By the way, questions have question marks.

The lack of ending quote marks makes me feel like I'm listening to the one-armed man from *The Fugitive* and he's making air quotes.

Stamp Out and Abolish Redundancy

Dear Student,

If there was an award for redundancy you would win the gold medal, the blue ribbon, the crown, the trophy, the title, and be the champion.

For every redundant pairing: "thoughts and ideas," "feelings and emotions," "words and vocabulary" –I want to cry.

Pro Tip: You don't use both "in the United States" and "in America" in the same sentence. Redundant and repetitive.

How are "the causes and reasons" different? Good luck explaining that to me.

You do not need to remind me on at the top of page two what you said three times on page one.

You wrote "you are honest and trustworthy." If you are trustworthy, you would have to be honest, but not necessarily a good writer.

You talk about "day to day," "agency to agency," and "jurisdiction to jurisdiction." I see a pattern, do you?

"As already discussed . . . " You've discussed this topic to death. Are you going to perform an autopsy to find out why it died?

This paper is two pages long. Do not say "as previously discussed". I may be old, but I'm not senile yet.

Clichés

Dear Student,

I see you're fluent in cliché, "Help them to get back on track and become productive citizens of society."

"When people work together a lot can be accomplished." Maybe you should write greeting cards rather than research papers.

"I figure this way is appropriate . . ." well . . . this isn't even an appropriate way to start a sentence. Colloquialisms much?

I see you already have a Master's degree in clichés. ". . . in any way, shape, or form." Cringe!

There are few things in academia as cliché as "living document". Unless you are writing on a pet; it's only a piece of paper.

I see that you not only write in American English, you are also fluent in jargon.

Typos

Dear Student,

Did Scooby-Do help you with this PowerPoint? "I plan to integrate data from revious models."

"First responders may have to prioritize providing case to the injured who in juries are more or less serious and survivable." Survive a jury?

Spelling Counts

Dear Student,

wipes tear from eye If you are going to misspell a word, try to avoid leaving out the "o" in "count."

Unless you're also from the UK, when you spell *centers* as "centres" it probably means you're plagiarizing.

When creating a figure, you still need to check the spelling of text. I'm not sure whether to laugh or cry. "Firemom?"

Those wavy colored lines in your document means something is wrong. The words are not *color surfing*.

If you're going to use the word 'druthers in your paper, you need to place the apostrophe in front of the word. Although if I had my 'druthers, you won't.

Stop using spell check as your proofreader! You mean "questions" not "question's". For the love of grammar!

Writing Mechanics

Dear Student,

Pro Tip–When writing a research paper: pick a tense and stick with it! I feel like I am on the TARDIS.

The upside of writing a terrible paper is that you'll never be suspected of plagiarizing.

It was easy to tell where you were quoting. Those were the grammatically correct sentences.

Not all words ending with an "s" are possessive. Some are plural. I do appreciate that you vary where you place the apostrophe, now follow the rules.

Your essay may be the longest, and worst, paragraph I have ever read. Seriously.

Your first sentence was so long, I began skimming the page for the period. It was hiding at the end of the paragraph.

Please write in paragraphs. I am sure you heard about them in school. Maybe fifth grade?

Capitalization

Dear Student,

Grading your Paper with its Random Capitalization takes me Back to kindergarten And games of duck, duck, Goose.

"Perhaps a solution is the Design/Methodology/approach." Your arbitrary capitalization is hurting my brain. There. Are. Rules.

Grading your paper enlightened me to my hatred of random capitals. I'll be talking about this with my therapist and bartender.

You have capital letters where they don't belong and don't have capital letters where you need them. Does one of your relatives own the local liquor store?

I'm so glad you aren't randomly capitalizing words. But the random use of boldface is hardly an improvement.

One requirement was that the your paper be formatted according to the style manual. I am not grading something written in ALL CAPS.

I can't decide if my annoyance at your random capitalization of words is due to undiagnosed OCD condition or just a hatred of randomness.

That's Not A Sentence

Dear Student,

When you have a sentence that is more than ninety-eight words, the chances are you have more than one sentence.

This sentence is 92 words long. I have written abstracts that were shorter! Dear God man, find the period key.

Most sentences are not six lines long. Please use more periods. They cost no more than commas and are healthier for your grade.

You have set a new record. One sentence with 134 words. This is sad, not impressive.

Chapter 6: Plagiarism

I have been finding plagiarism in my students' writing long before we had plagiarism checkers. I can usually "hear" changes in voice that indicate a change in authorship. Plagiarism checkers have made it easier to find the copy-and-paste style of writing and even provide a percentage of similarity between the student's paper and their sources. While most students would never cheat by copying exam answers off the person next to them, the same students often fail to understand that plagiarism is another form of cheating.

There's a Whole Lot of Quoting Going On

Dear Student,

Your paper is like a patchwork quilt. You have stitched together quotations from multiple sources. Where are your words?

Paraphrasing means to put it in your own words with your own structure. Changing every fourth word is just word substitution.

You are not allowed to quote over 170 words from this article. I will send your grade to the authors.

Cut and Paste Artists

Dear Student,

Do you even know what "in your own words" means? You couldn't prove it by this paper.

After reading pages of opinions, you shocked me when you said something intelligent supported by citations. Who wrote that?

Pro Tip: If your professor is also an author, don't tell the professor that plagiarizing isn't *really* stealing. My words are my product.

Thanks for the laughs. Your request to *forget* the academic dishonesty sanctions was almost as funny as your total lack of remorse.

Getting an A on a paper you didn't write should give you as much satisfaction as getting a medal for a race you didn't run.

I'll treasure those emails you sent about what a great instructor I am. Especially now that I've failed you for plagiarizing.

Thanks for the laughs. I hope you will enjoy explaining why you plagiarized your post about ethics.

Calling me unethical for failing you when you plagiarized the last two assignments reaches a new level of chutzpah.

I cannot evaluate your writing skills when you only wrote two sentences in your two page submission. Can you spell plagiarism?

I am not impressed by your grades in other classes and it is not a defense for plagiarism.

Pro Tip: Don't plagiarize the sample paper. I wrote it, and I can recognize my own writing.

You remembered twenty-seven words in a row from the article but you forgot the citation? Do you really expect me to believe that?

Yes, you had the minimum number of words in your paper. However, sixty percent of them were not *your* words.

I found seventeen words on five pages that you wrote. How do I grade the word "and"?

You began every sentence with an "ing" word for two pages. Now I find this well-written paragraph. I wonder who wrote it.

Recyclers

Self-plagiarism has become a "thing" in academia. Journals require that authors cite their previous research if they use them in new manuscripts. Students are prohibited from submitting the same papers to multiple courses. This is called "dual submission" or "recycling" and is another form of academic dishonesty.

Dear Student,

My first clue that you didn't write this paper for my class is that it's in Chicago style, and we use APA style.

My second clue your paper wasn't written for this class is that you have no subject headings. There were required headings for this assignment.

My third clue: key words are missing, such as problem, purpose, and ethics.

Finally, research proposals must *propose research.* The only thing proposed by your paper was your failing grade.

I'm searching for a word that describes recycling a paper reported for plagiarism earlier this term. Lazy? Stupid? Apathetic?

Ninety-nine percent similarity means you only change the course number and the professor's name.

The file properties on your paper say you began writing this paper last year. Wow, that's either evidence of psychic powers or dual submission.

I hope you got a good grade on this paper when you used it before. Too bad it doesn't fit with this assignment.

Your paper on copyright law wasn't *bad,* but it's too bad copyright law had nothing to do with the assignment.

When you write a bad sentence in your introduction and then use the exact sentence again on later pages, I notice.

I have no idea how to grade this paper since it is for another class. The other professor's name on the cover page was a dead giveaway.

Sorry, you're going to have to write on a correct topic rather than the one you've been milking in all your previous classes.

The Plagiarism Checker

Dear Student,

Just what did you think the ninety percent similarity report from the plagiarism checker meant? Great minds think alike?

You plagiarized so much in your paper, the plagiarism checker's report began with "Not again!"

Dear Student

Thank you for cutting and pasting your way through this assignment. I really enjoy filling out those academic dishonesty forms.

Chapter 7: Scholarly Writing

The Style Manual

Every discipline has a style manual, which specifies how papers should be written. In graduate school, the style manual takes on a new level of importance as the students are moving to becoming more scholarly in their professions. Unfortunately, most students only consult the style manual for how to format a reference. And some students don't even do that.

Dear Student,

    Love what you did with your spacing. It was so light and airy. Truly artistic. Next time, follow the style manual.

Your haphazard approach to the format of your references reminds me of a Pollock painting. Drips of italics and punctuation.

Please provide the style manual page number where it tells you to change the font color for emphasis. That's what I thought.

For the love of my eyesight, pick a font and stay with it . . . but not Comic Sans or Papyrus.

I will be happy to help you with style manual formats. First tip, buy the manual. Second tip, look it up. You're welcome.

Spacing is not trivial. "The pen is mightier than the sword." Removing the space before "is" changes the entire sentence!

If you don't define the acronym, I get to. Today FEMA means "Flying Exotic Male Acrobats." That will make reading your paper a lot of fun!

You can't abbreviate "Expert Domestic Violence Courts with SDVCs. It makes no sense.

Have you ever met an acronym you didn't like? Now what did those letters mean again? *turns back to the first page*

Get Organized

Dear Student,

You bounce back and forth between your research study and the research problem so much I feel like I'm watching a tennis match.

Your paper makes Congress look organized and efficient.

There is this wonderful invention that improves clarity and organizes your points. It is called "the paragraph". Use it.

Trying to follow your logic was a lot like trying to follow a cat. No discernible goal, random directional shifts, and backtracking.

So is the "teeming network" bigger than the "slew" of problems? Wow. You really have quite the vocabulary of vague words.

References

Dear Student,

There's this invention called the alphabet. You probably remember it from the song you learned in kindergarten. It determines the order of your references.

Your reference page demonstrates a high amount of creative flare and a low amount of concern with the style manual.

It's too bad that Microsoft clip art isn't a peer-reviewed source because you are one shy of the minimum. No points for you!

Reference and citation formats are not optional. But don't worry, you can learn these formats when you take this course—again.

Nothing quite screams "Attitude" like a reference page that is nothing but URLs.

I just love hearing how you have been doing your references wrong for multiple terms. As Picard said, "The line must be drawn here!"

Citations

Dear Student,

Your lack of attention to the directions for this assignment was only surpassed by your complete disregard for the style formats.

Your article had two authors but you keep referring to the article only by the second author's name. Did the first author piss you off or something?

Pro Tip: Research papers are called research papers because you're supposed to do research. In other words, you MUST have citations!

When making statements in research papers, even people with Ph.D.s cite their sources. You only have B.S. (in more ways than one.)

If "several studies" have found this, where are the citations for this statement? I'm just supposed to trust you? No.

While attributing passages in your assignment, don't forget to cite the blogger whose analysis is your paper.

After grading five plagiarized papers in a row, this is "A" work. You might have crazy ideas, but at least they're your crazy ideas.

Excellent job on using original sources. However, I should fail you for citing "The National Enquirer." A little too original for graduate school.

Please keep in mind that citing the Bible is not recommended in this research methods course. God cannot be "peer-reviewed."

Chapter 8: Why Did You Do That?

Think About What You Are Saying

One of my students wrote: "Microsoft Windows is one of the most widely used operating systems with well over fifty-thousand lines of code and even though it has a high likelihood of crashing, businesses and homes all over the country find themselves using it." I immediately thought to myself, this kind of thing happens every day to me. One minute I'm cooking dinner, and the next minute I find myself using Windows. I have no idea how this happens.

Dear Student,

    Yes, I found myself using Microsoft Windows tonight. I have no idea how this happened.

I love research because I like discovering patterns. Research papers are not supposed to read like a stream of consciousness.

If you have two exclusive actions, don't use "and/or." You can't abuse a drug and then sell it illegally. Think about it.

The voice in your post was so passive, I wondered if it was written by your Golden Retriever.

"It is extremely important for the worker to know and learn Microsoft windows inside out and backwards . . . " Explain this to me, why would you learn something backwards?

Your case for how single-parent homes lead to delinquency wasn't supported by your example of a killer reared by two parents.

"Parenting Classes for both children and mother" So, let me get this straight, the children need parenting classes?

Thanks for the mental image: "especially for departments that are left sitting on hundreds of unidentified bodies." New seat please.

"Issues that can send a juvenile over the bridge and live a life of criminal behavior" Let's just burn the bridge!

"They can keep up with the drugs . . ." Didn't know drugs could run as fast as people.

Unless he used a TARDIS, the author writing in 1960 did not cite the author writing in 2007.

"Many of today's juvenile court systems are collapsing under their own weight." Fat courts?

On occasion I have felt great. How does one "greatly feel?" What does that even mean?

When you wrote "this area of study is a passion of mine" I wasn't impressed, I was mortified. Have you tried porn?

"The data that you receive from this research will fuel your research to the next level." Explosive data, please stand back!

"This theory will get you all of the answers that you need for your research and reliable answers." I am speechless.

I cannot believe you just ruined your paper by saying "YOLO" in your conclusion. Really? In graduate school?

Believe it or not, theorists are people. "Throughout time there has been many people and theorists who try . . ."

Thanks for letting me know this student's post was new and informative. Too bad he posted the transcript to the video you said you watched.

Did you look at the publication date? When you use the word "currently," you should cite research less than ten years old.

How do you calculate the number of unreported cases? If they are unreported . . .

"Everybody knows" includes my neighbor's six-week-old baby. Trust me, she knows very little.

Be careful about blanket statements. If you say all redshirts died, and I find one who lived (like Scotty) you look like an idiot.

PowerPoint Slides

Dear Student,

Assigning projects in PowerPoint is a clever means of forcing students to summarize. I see you cannot be forced.

Why do you have so many words on these PowerPoint slides? Are you trying to make me blind? Use bullets. Slay the wordiness monster!

There is special place in hell for people who use ten point, Monotype Corsiva, as their font on PowerPoint slides.

Having two title slides in your presentation is not a great way to start off, unless you don't want an A.

When figures on your PowerPoint slides are black, it's particularly "artsy" of you to write across them with a black font. Artsy, but not smart.

Your smooth rendition of your previous paper on your PowerPoint slides speaks volumes about your skills with PowerPoint and boring people.

When the final project is created in PowerPoint. I don't expect to see "Click to add title" on any slides of an A student. Just a hint.

Thanks for letting me know to view your PowerPoint in slide show mode. Heaven forbid I'd have missed those animated gifs.

A PowerPoint slide is not the same thing as a page. You took so many words to come to your point that your point is now dull.

What Part of?

Dear Student,

What part of "required" didn't you understand? It doesn't mean the same thing as "optional" or "if you feel like it."

What part of "proposal" didn't you understand? You aren't supposed to do the research, just tell me what you want to do.

What part of "due date" didn't you understand? The "date" part or the "due" part?

What part of "summarize" didn't you understand? Summaries are supposed to be shorter than the original material.

Chapter 9: This is Graduate School

Welcome to Graduate School

Dear Student,

There's a special place in hell for magazines that pretend to be scholarly journals. Sorry you fell for their trap.

I know this is confusing, but you're in graduate school and it's time to learn the differences among "too", "to", and "two."

If you continue in graduate school you'll have several new experiences to look forward to (i.e. Rx for anxiety and depression.)

Trying to get through graduate school by cheating and finding loopholes will limit your job opportunities to Congressman.

This is graduate school. Cut and paste was kindergarten. Grow up!

I am like OMG about your IMHO post. You do realize you are in graduate school and not on Twitter, don't you?

You Don't Belong in Graduate School

Dear Student,

It is apparent you are not going to let my instructions interfere with your performance on this assignment.

You remind me of the guy who couldn't pour water out of a boot when the instructions were written on the heel.

If you ever see a job ad looking for an expert at cutting and pasting, be sure to ask me for a letter of recommendation.

I'm sorry to hear that the stress of this semester is about to give you "a nervous brake down." Maybe you should stop.

"According to LegalDefinition.com . . . " You have got to be kidding me!

I understand social media. Just don't post to Facebook during my lectures. I don't walk around the room for exercise.

I am going to assume that was a typo and not a winky-face. Otherwise, the horror of it would just be too much for me.

The Power of Proofreading!

Dear Student,

Sloppy doesn't begin to describe someone who doesn't spell the name of the author correctly. It was only five letters long!

Where is the rest of this sentence? "I must say I enjoyed your very honest."

There is this thing called "proofreading" that prevents your post from looking like your cat walked across your keyboard.

That's the fourth typo on the first page! If you aren't going to read your own writing, why should I?

Only proofreading will allow to "see" where you went "wee".

Spell Check

Dear Student,

You should have considered sharing authorship of this paper with spell check.

I love independent thinkers; except for the ones who ignore spell-check.

If you put "ect" on a slide, you had better mean "electroconvulsive therapy" not "etc." It's shocking you'd make this error.

"Lightning" is not the same thing as "lightening". Spell check will not help you.

Obviously, your skills do not include the use of spell check. "I plan to use a quantitative methoed."

You meant you "applauded the effort." You wrote that you "appalled the effort." Spell check will not save you from that one.

Spell check fails again. "The model asserts that income is commiserate with the skills of the occupation." The word is *commensurate*.

Spell check won't catch everything, but that doesn't mean you shouldn't use it.

Spell check wasn't your friend. When you said "show skills" you meant "social skills". Who knows what you typed.

". . . officers do not have appropriate experiment to handle sex offenders" You meant "experience." Spell check can't help!

What Were You Thinking?

Dear Student,

There is a name for students who call without an appointment and then call me by my first name. It sounds like "idiot."

I wish I knew an adequate penalty for putting :) in a research paper. But I'm too busy crying to think of one. *sobbing*

"Never in a billion years . . ." Exaggeration is a million times worse than understatement.

Before becoming a professor, I would stop and help turtles cross the street. I still help turtles, but students, you're on your own.

I just love it when your final project includes all the same errors I identified on your previous assignments. I'd hate to see anything new.

How many appointments do you think you can miss before I stop giving you appointments? Let's compare numbers.

Word Dripping in Sarcasm

Dear Student,

Of course I like you. I spent extra time helping you out and you ignored all my advice. What's not to like?

I don't view sarcasm as part of my job. It's more of a job perk.

Loved the creative spacing in your paper. You might want to consider a career in graphic arts rather than writing research papers.

Your paper was a joy to read. I loved your random capitalizations as much as the sprinkling of bold type.

I had no idea you were on a first name basis with the Secretary of the Department of Human Services. I only refer to her by her last name.

Please tell me how I should grade your paper. Obviously, my years of experience and PhD are no match for your opinion.

Stupid

Dear Student,

In case you didn't notice, online courses aren't like campus courses. You can't slide a late assignment under my door and hope I won't know when you turned it in.

When citing works of famous psychologists, it's important to spell the name correctly or you look like an idiot. "Mashlow?"

I just took fifteen minutes explaining this assignment. When you asked, "So what are we doing?" a small part of me died.

Before turning in a paper you stole off "http://freeessays.com" you might want to remove the hyperlink to make it more challenging.

Don't ask for an extension on due date and plead "hangover" as the rationale. Really? Better to plead "stupid".

If I killed you for writing in ALL CAPS, there isn't a jury in this country who would convict me. I might even get a medal.

Insults

Dear Student,

The last time I saw writing of this quality it was printed . . . in crayon.

I will not answer your email. I never argue with an idiot. You'll drag me down to your level and beat me with your experience.

I can explain it to you, but I can't understand it for you.

If convoluted logic were a sport, you could be in the Olympics!

Your paper was written at a level I have rarely seen before. Probably because I don't teach third grade.

I've always been able to say nice things about a student's paper no matter how poorly written. I really liked your font.

Your advisor says you're upset by the penalty you received for plagiarism. Can you spell "boo-hoo" or do you need to cut and paste that too?

I see you are bilingual in English and gibberish. I only know English.

When you said you're "like literally" about to die. Like and literally are opposites. Which makes this an oxymoron. Like you.

Chapter 10: You Said What?

Did You Read What You Wrote?

Dear Student,

"The subject of life imprisonment and executions appears to be a controversial matter in our society." Understatement much?

How do you compare the cost *effectiveness* of lifetime in prison versus execution? Effective doing what?

I have never heard of police or people referred to as "law enforcers" . . . outside of Star Trek.

"Sentencing guidelines are a direct result of wasteful spending on behalf of the criminal justice system." Citation? I didn't think so.

"Social Workers Designated in/out of Prison to assist with inmates." Were the social workers in prison for bad grammar?

"... the leader wanting to serve, nurture, and grow their staff" put my mind right in the gutter.

You've stumped the Internet. "Reprocitions" doesn't appear to be a word in any language. You didn't even leave context clues.

"Most minorities and many liberals feel police department policies illegally profile them because they are Black."

"Them being labeled offends them in some kind of way and the way that they react is in deviant ways and crimes." Grammar much?

"... officers may be biased against sex offenders." If they're police officers isn't that their job?

"The only person to blame for overcrowding in jails is the offender." Criminal justice is not a good choice for your career.

"When confronted with a corpse . . ." I didn't realize the dead could confront anyone.

Are you referring to altitude or latitude? "Having being raised up in lower parts of a town there has always been labeling."

"I was very shocked knowing finding out these very same outcomes." Uh? Translation please?

". . . there are not enough eyes to accommodate each of the inmates present." Gruesome image. Do you want the inmates to share eyes?

There is no "elevation of caseloads" . . . unless you are moving them to Denver.

Do you really believe this? "Criminals walk streets thinking about the debate between exact science and archaeological interpretation."

". . . investigators have boxes filled with unsolved crimes and missing persons." There are people in their boxes?

You wrote "A scientific breakthrough that came to life around the 1800's . . . " are you talking about Frankenstein's monster?

"Returning prisoners contribute significantly to the high rate of prisoners currently in prison." Where do I begin?

"However, local management awareness is very in communicating information to the citizens in their communities." WTF? WTF? WTF? W . . .

"A few dangers this group faces are, weaving an eight-thousand pound vehicle through congested traffic...." Shouldn't they be driving it?

You can take refuge "in" a car or "behind" a car. How does one take refuge "with" a car? Have you been watching Disney movies?

"Then they will start to do whatever pops up in their heads." If you have popping in your head, you need to see a doctor.

When you said "The world has to be prepared for whatever will come." Please cite the sci-fi movie. Please cite something!

I wouldn't make an ethical decision based on, "If my grandmother were watching, what would I do?" You don't know my granny!

I'm glad you having a wild time! "I have found this class to be very challenging but in the end will be worth wild."

Compliments, maybe

Dear Student,

    I can't say I miss your wordy and repetitive explanations. Your final project rocks. Now if you could only learn to cite . . . .

    You are shooting citations off like a real cowboy. Your writing is as smooth as a baby's butt. What has gotten into you?

    Congratulations on earning 100% on your paper. Considering how your peers did, you may want to consider hiring a bodyguard.

    While entering your grade of one-hundred percent, I admit to doing the Calvin and Hobbes Happy Dance. But no one saw me, so it doesn't count.

    This paper is so well written I'm pinching myself because I'm afraid I'm dreaming. Turning to page two. Do *not* screw this up!

I just loved your use of citations. I hope you can make it a fashion trend that catches on with the rest of the class.

You read my comments on the file. You sent me questions ahead of our phone conference. You called on time. Are sure you're my student?

Quoting the syllabus to me is a great way to make me smile.

Responses to Student Emails

Dear Student,

Thanks for the email. You're right, that sentence is a good problem statement. Too bad that sentence wasn't in your paper.

I'm denying your request to "wipe out" your plagiarism sanctions. I'm keeping your email so I can be mad at you all over again.

Thanks for your email complaining how you didn't "mean to" plagiarize. Can't wait for you to request for a letter of recommendation.

While reading your email complaining about the plagiarism checker requirement, I had to resist an urge to reach for one of my dog's poo bags.

Pro Tip: Rather than sending an apology email about your previous email, don't email rants to your professor. Ask questions.

Sorry it took twelve hours to answer email. Believe it or not . . . this professor has a life! Sincerely, never-to-be-tenured professor.

In response to your email about improving your grade . . . you might try reading the directions!

So, You Want to be My Graduate Assistant?

Dear Student,

Being a "booth-babe" at a Comic Con is not a professional presentation. But thanks for the laughs.

I can see your great attention to detail in the way you misspelled my name.

Being a volunteer for a drug trial is not the same thing as having conducted research. You were the lab rat.

Please explain how your work at the bookstore on campus makes you qualified to help me with my research. Clerks are not librarians.

If your introduction email says that my research has peeked your interest, then were not a good fit.

When I Say . . .

When I say that you should go back and check something, that means you did it wrong.

When I say that you have a good start on something, that means your paper isn't finished yet.

When I say that you need to proofread, it means that you had more typos than I do when I try to Tweet without my glasses.

When I said "unidentified and improperly cited quotations" this is a kinder term for plagiarism.

When I have to say "according to who?" more than fifteen times on the first page it means you are not citing enough research.

When I say on your paper "Please explain." It is only because I am too nice to say "what the fuck does that mean?"

When I say "APA error" on your paper that means you did it wrong. No, I don't tell you what the error is so you will *look it up*.

Chapter 11: Bad News

Peer Reviewed

Dear Student,

Why in heaven's name would you think a book was the same as a peer-reviewed article? I may never believe a word you say again.

When you asked me if I just want peer-reviewed journals or if I also want peer-reviewed articles—a small part of me died.

No, it is not because I'm old or have a PhD that I know the journal is not peer-reviewed. It's because I looked it up. Why didn't you know?

I was impressed when you told me you didn't need help finding peer-reviewed articles . . . until I read your references section.

You work at a library and don't know differences between peer-reviewed articles and magazine articles? My nightmares will be your fault!

Can't wait to read your email about how you don't understand how your list of twenty websites didn't satisfy the ten peer-reviewed articles requirement.

The lack of peer-reviewed articles in your research paper makes me wonder if you know what they are, or are afraid of them.

"It is important to review the literature . . . because you want to be certain the literature is credible." Heard of peer reviews?

If you don't know how to find peer-reviewed articles, you're playing with fire by only using the minimum number of references.

Excuses

Dear Student,

Lots of things that aren't peer-reviewed articles can be found in the library. Magazines, books, and trash are a few examples.

Death is no excuse for missing class. Unless it is yours.

They're called "annual conferences" because they're held every year. So why is it an excuse that you were attending one when the assignment was due?

This week only, I will accept as an excuse "I went to see Star Trek Into Darkness." Priorities.

If you used as much brain power on your papers as you do on your excuses for why it's late, you'd get better grades.

A Halloween party is not a good reason to miss class. It may be the honest reason, but you might think of another explanation.

Irony

Dear Student,

There is a sick kind of irony about plagiarizing your example of the ethics failure of a fellow police officer.

I promise I'll never forget you. The irony that you would plagiarize your ethics post from my own blog is beyond description!

I hope you appreciate the irony that a student I charged with academic dishonesty is calling me unethical. I do.

Only You

Dear Student,

You are the only one who was surprised. "Surprisingly, theoretical frameworks are also important in exploratory studies"

Since you are the only one having this problem it isn't the website. The problem is between the seat and the keyboard.

I am sorry about the loss of your aunt. I cannot grade six weeks of your missed work in the next two weeks, or my family would lose me.

I've emailed you. I've called your advisor. I've posted on the discussion board. Will you PLEASE stop writing in all capital letters?

Course requirements do not change based on your job, family, other courses, addictions, hair color, religion, commute, etc.

Thank you for submitting such an entertaining assignment. It was funny—as if you never came to class.

If I were "impossible to please", then half of the class would not have earned As.

When the quiz is "open book" it means you should bring your book to class. No, I will not loan you mine.

Chapter 12: Grades and Grading

Don't Bother Me, I'm Grading

Dear Student,

While grading papers I channel Fox Mulder. "I want to believe" but I "trust no one."

I provided seven headings and you used three. I feel like I'm on a bloody scavenger hunt. Let's hope I don't miss anything.

I won't get all the early papers graded tonight. I'm going to my RPG for a few hours. I am entitled to have a (geeky) life.

Yes. I knew what you meant, but I can only grade what you wrote.

While discussing your grade, please keep in mind the number of times I wrote "This is not a sentence" on your paper.

I'm sorry my comment bubbles are red. They make your paper look like it was the scene of a horrible massacre.

"It is imperative to read the information you are researching . . . " You actually read that stuff? Could have fooled me.

When you don't follow the instructions for the paper, it doesn't take all that long to grade. F is for Fast.

I just spent more time grading your paper than you probably did writing it.

When you miss the point of the research question, there really isn't much you will get right in the rest of your paper.

If you thought the sheer volume of grading would mean I would only skim your work, that would be your second mistake.

I don't grade effort. I don't read between the lines. I only grade the BLACK part of the page.

Read the Instructions

Dear Student,

When I said you could go over the ten to twelve slides, that didn't mean I'd grade thirty-seven.

Nice annotated bibliography; too bad I hadn't assigned one. Loved: "Here is my literature review, in no particular order."

Thank you for turning your paper in early. However, you could have spent the extra time *reading the directions.*

Your paper is proof that every time I try to make my instructions fool-proof, I underestimate the foolishness of fools.

I can hardly wait to hear your request for extra credit. But why should I believe you would follow those directions either?

When you don't follow the directions, turning your work in early only means I have a lot of time to find all the errors. Thanks.

You ignored my suggested headings. If you don't like your grade, you won't mind if I ignore you, will you?

Being concise is one thing. Turning in 245 words for a 1,200 word paper is called something else. It's called "fail".

Your paper reads as though you can't.

You would do better on your assignments if you actually read the directions. P.S. I hope you're not assembling any toys in December.

You have to answer the questions on the assignment. You don't get to make up your own. What a concept.

When your professor assigns a two to three page paper, do not turn in ten pages! Extra pages will not earn you extra points.

Your claim that the missing assignment elements were actually present in your paper means you must be using a Romulan cloaking device as well as bad writing.

Read The Syllabus

Dear Student,

I'm sorry you did not realize your discussion post would be graded. Did you read the syllabus? That's what I thought.

You posted that you read the syllabus, but you did not follow the hidden instructions. Can you spell *liar*?

The last week of the term is *not* when you should tell me you finally found the syllabus. It was online all term.

If I re-named the syllabus "Course FAQ" would you read it then? Sigh.

The late policy is clearly stated in my syllabus, but you wouldn't know that because . . . well . . . *reading*.

I think our relationship has moved beyond the "did you read the syllabus?" phase to the "get a clue" phase.

I wonder if I renamed my syllabus, "How to Survive the Zombie grading Apocalypse" would you read it then?

When you say you read the attached syllabus, and I forgot to attach it, can you guess who looks worse?

What on earth is so difficult about reading the syllabus? You want other languages? YouTube video? Music? Interpretive dance?

Read

Dear Student,

How can you be surprised that I know when you are quoting from the book? Not only did I assign the book, I read it too.

I'm sorry the video won't play on your computer, but there's a transcript. You can read, can't you?

Did you read any of my 147 comments on your paper? If you want me to explain your grade, you should start by asking a question.

Finding out what is available in your field is not research. It is called "reading." Obviously, that's a new concept for you.

Why didn't you read the assigned articles? Why am I grading this? Assigned means required.

You were assigned one chapter and three articles for this post. Please explain why you used your dictionary.

When I can answer all your questions by identifying the page in the book with the information . . . guess what that tells me about you?

I am not your parent, IT help desk, proofreader, librarian, tutor, or Google. I'm only your professor. Read the syllabus.

CHAPTER 13: IT'S MY JOB

Yes, I Check

Dear Student,

So, you don't think there are many studies on your topic? I found 120,000 articles on Google Scholar because I looked!

Apparently, you didn't expect me to read the online obituary you sent. Your name was not listed. Please explain.

We use "n.d." on articles without publication dates. Your article was published in 2008. I know because *I looked it up*.

Only list references for works you cite in your paper. With the find feature of Word, it is easy to check.

Grades and Grave Concerns

Dear Student,

I didn't realize we were at the "I'll-do-anything-to-improve-my-grade" day in the course. *Checks calendar* Yep, three days left.

I am sorry to hear about how you're suffering in my course. I can empathize because I suffer when I grade your work.

There really isn't a reason to care about your grade any more. Your final project is a witness to your apathy. Typo-city.

So you finally realized if you hadn't skipped those posts, your grade would be better. No, you can't go back without a time machine.

I don't give grades; students earn them. In spite of my best efforts you have earned an F.

Needing to grade something twice makes me cranky. Having a student demand I do it "right away" is a poor strategy. Think about it.

Do not email me a draft of your paper to "look over". I don't pre-grade anything. I'm not the writing lab.

I respect your right to fail. If it was your goal to fail, then you have succeeded.

There is one week left in the term. You are missing half the assignments. Why are you surprised you are failing? Well. Surprise!

How is it that I am to blame for your grade? You earned that grade. You wrote the paper, didn't you?

I am *not* trying to fail you. You are doing that all on your own.

I know this may come as a shock to you, but I don't give points for "trying."

The more I grade papers, the more I miss going to the dentist.

Too Late

Dear Student,

You want extra time because the assignment was due on Mothers' Day? Did you fly halfway around the world to see her? No? Then, no.

You'll never know just how much I regret that I can't accept your assignment which you turned in ten days late. Or how little.

You submitted your paper two weeks late— even after I said I wouldn't accept it. I'm good at ignoring. My cat has trained me well.

Just because I hadn't put a zero in the gradebook before now, it doesn't mean you could still turn in this paper that was due five weeks ago.

Turning in an assignment eight days late warrants a little more explanation than "I've had a rough semester." Me too

If you don't think deadlines are important, next year try filing your tax return on April 16th.

Of course I don't mind you just turned in a paper two weeks late without an explanation. Your grade won't need one either.

Of course you turned in your assignments "when you could." Next time turn them in "when you should." Hello late penalty.

The semester is over. Don't even think you can submit any more work late. Well, you can think it. Just don't try it.

I grade the papers which are submitted on time first. Your work was three weeks late. Like you, I'm "sorry for the inconvenience."

A+ for chutzpah - telling me you won't submit your last assignment because you don't like your previous grades.

They're called deadlines because of what happens to your grade when you miss them.

This assignment is two weeks late and you want it graded in less than twenty-four hours? Why? And no.

No. I will not give you more time for the assignment. Shopping is not an unforeseen emergency. *rolls eyes*

Incompletes

Dear Student,

Giving you an incomplete is like grounding my teenager. I will be the only one suffering!

An "incomplete" is given when you can't turn in the work due to illness, etc. Your plagiarized work was turned in.

Against my better judgment, I'll give you an incomplete. Do not ask for extensions on deadlines. Notice I didn't say due dates.

Extra Credit

Dear Student,

You haven't done the work and it's too late to catch up. There's only one word that describes your extra credit request. Nuts!

All extra credit requires the use of a TARDIS to go back to the start of the term and then you must do the work on time.

If you were falsely accused of murder, would you hire a lawyer to defend you who got through law school on extra credit?

No extra credit. You haven't turned anything in on time all term. Term ends Friday. No. Extra. Credit. No.

The only extra credit projects I allow involve Star Trek technology. Can you build a transporter?

Write it Again, Sam

Dear Student,

If you want a third rewrite, you will need to make a convincing argument. Something other than you just don't like your grade.

I am not disappointed you *passed* on the re-write opportunity. I hope you're not disappointed in your final grade.

You probably should not have reminded me this is your third attempt.

Your re-write is so good you either: (A) went to the writing center or (B) paid someone to write it for you.

Why didn't you fix all the errors before submitting your re-write? They didn't magically become correct when you resubmitted.

Do not submit an assignment and call it your "first attempt". No. You only get one attempt. This is it.

No. There are no penalty-free re-writes. Fairness to all students means no one gets a second chance for an A.

Do The Math

Dear Student,

Pro Tip: When three questions are asked, I am looking for three answers.

When discussing the "current situation," please cite research that is less than thirty years old.

When the minimum requirement is a 100 word response, why did you write 22? I know this isn't a math class, but it is graduate school.

I'm sorry to hear how you salved over the last assignment. Apparently you were earning one point per hour.

Chapter 14: "You'll Never Be a Researcher"

That's Your Opinion

Dear Student,

"Qualitative data methods deal with feeling and other non-researchable elements." My qualitative colleagues are going to be shocked.

I'm so glad you demonstrated your professional detachment in your paper about *broken* families. Biased much?

"Poor ethical choices are made by alcoholic police officers." I'm so relieved you are a totally objective researcher.

"This research comprehensively examines the lack of effectiveness . . . " Where were you when we were discussing research bias?

"Qualitative procedures can be problematic as well as erroneous." Really? Not everyone shares your opinion . . . or bias.

I just love reading unsubstantiated claims about research gaps. They're almost as fun as your criticism of traditional methods.

Do you know the difference between a research question and a rhetorical question? Do you even care?

I'm guessing this rant is your problem statement. First, I shouldn't have to guess. Second, this shouldn't read like a rant.

While this idea may be new to you, if you look over the last fifty years of studies, you will find someone beat you to it. In fact, a lot of someones.

I'm sure your friends value your opinion. In graduate school, we value research. Back up your statements with citations.

"Our youth are the back bones of our nation." Says you. I think middle-aged video game players are our backbone. Opinion war!

That's Not How It Works

Dear Student,

"Qualitative research wishes to answer the question . . . " Wishes? Since when do we use genies?

Proposing one research study that will take your "entire career to conduct" isn't noble, it is rather silly. Think about it.

If you don't know the difference between a problem and a purpose, then you will live an interesting life.

Don't use words such as "feel" when writing about research. We base our conclusions on observations, not emotions.

Please say something new. Anything. "to gather important facts and data gathering . . . "

Your research topic and key words should be congruent. Yours are not even in the same time zone.

Random sampling is not a sloppy method. It's not like your random thoughts . . .

PhDs and Academics

Dear Student,

A Ph.D. is not called a terminal degree because you die from it. I don't think . . . but now that you mention it . . . .

I had no trouble understanding your points. I am fluent in gibberish, lingo, and obfuscation. After all, I am an academic!

Considering all the work of my dissertation and the student loans to pay for my Ph.D., the least you can do is call me "doctor".

You never answered the question. What you wrote was a lot of double-talk. I know double-talk when I see it. I'm a professor!

"What's the best part of being an adjunct?" Not getting phone calls from my students' mommies. Been there. Done that.

"More is known about what doesn't work than what does." I want to cry.

Really? "Issues have arisen?" Do tell. I mean that. Tell me what the issues are. This is a research paper!

If this was easy, everyone would do it. Then everyone would have PhDs. Think about it.

Just because you're older than me, doesn't mean you know more. My PhD trumps your BS in more ways than one.

Statistics

Dear Student,

Citations to "Kirk" actually refer to the author of a stats book, not the captain of the USS Enterprise.

You have some unbelievable statistics in your paper. They might be believable if you cited your source.

Chapter 15: Leftover Musings

Twitter

Dear Student,

I almost didn't grade your late assignment, but I needed funny stuff to tweet. Win-Win. well, actually you didn't pass, but I got retweeted.

If you thought I was harsh with the comments on your paper, you wouldn't believe what I wrote about you on Twitter!

I understand procrastination. I've been on Twitter, Facebook, and alphabetized my soup cans today to avoid grading papers.

Thanks so much for this paper. Your paper now sets the record for the source of the highest number of tweets.

Your post was well written and reflective. It followed the discussion question. Basically, you gave me nothing to tweet about!

No, I am not the same person tweeting about the mistakes in your papers. Someone does that?

Try writing the purpose statement for your research like a tweet. Only 140 characters allowed, but no smiley faces.

My teacher gift guide:
    K-5=Apple
    6-9=Valium
    10-12=Chocolate
    Undergraduate =Starbucks
    Graduate school=Scotch
    PhD program =work hard and finish

Dammit Jim, I'm Your Professor Not A . . .

Dear Student,

I am your professor, not your confessor. Tell me what you need or want, not how you feel!

Your email to the IT help desk somehow came to my inbox. Obviously, you don't think I am going to fix your computer problem.

Why are you asking me about Word formats? Do I look like Google?

I Have A Life

Dear Student,

I appreciate all *details* you provided about the drama going on in your life. I won't sleep for days. By the way, what did you want?

I am sorry if I take more than a day to respond to your nonsense. I am easily dis—oh, look . . . a squirrel!

I will be unavailable this weekend owing to my attendance at a comic con—I mean conference.

Sure I will grade your late paper tonight. It's not like I have a life or anything.

Seven am on a Saturday is not a reasonable time to call. Sorry you must go to work early. Your problems are not my problems.

You're Driving Me to Drink

Dear Student,

Thanks for the email. Thanks to you, my AA sponsor has offered to buy me more Scotch!

When grading a stack of papers, the ones at the bottom usually get higher grades. Grading drift? Intoxication? You decide.

My lack of comments on your paper has more to do with impairments caused by strong drink than your notable insights.

Of course, I drink while grading. Even you haven't read this paper sober, I can tell.

In order to consider your paper A work, I would have to be too drunk to grade it.

I have run out of scotch, and therefore, must wait until tomorrow to finish grading your paper. There's no way I can do this sober!

The reason your classmate got a better grade is either because I like her better, or I had more to drink when I graded her paper.

Now That You Mentioned It . . .

Dear Student,

Your citation of Maslow (1943) has me wondering where he would have placed WiFi in his hierarchy of needs.

Your ability to make up facts and write them without citation has left me wondering. Have you ever run for a political office?

Bullshit and backspace can both be abbreviated "b.s." Coincidence? I think not.

I realize you call me "Professor" not out of respect, but because it makes you feel like you're in a Harry Potter movie!

I have been shaking my head so much while reading your paper, I don't think I will need to go to the gym this morning.

I don't need to hear all the details about your personal drama. I have a teenager, an ex-spouse, and a cat. Need I say more?

When you wrote "chaos rules" in your paper, my brain saw Agent 86 talking on his shoe phone.

"I believe the mental health profession has exploded into our society" Was that a *shrink* bomb?

I would give you a red shirt, but you would understand the message since you're too young to have watched Star Trek.

Pure Genius

At times, my students write the funniest stuff in their papers. Here are some real gems.
Dear Student,

"It is typically believed that it's easier to decide on a topic before starting to write a paper." Yep. That's the first step.

"There are many problems that are facing the world of today." You have a great grasp of the obvious.

"The economy plays a big role in the amount of spending in the United States" . . . and the sky is blue?

"Science is amazing in theory." You are hurting my brain.

Acknowledgements

This book came about because of the following I have on Twitter. To the people who follow my account, retweet me, and interact with me - Thank you. Most people put disclaimers on their accounts that say, "retweets do not equal endorsements." Or something close that. However, I have found that when I can make others chuckle at my "Dear Student" tweets, I see a large number of retweets.

I have the good fortune of belonging to local critique groups.

SW WA/OR Write to Publish. This critique group was founded by Linda Stirling, and she is the author of several books including her forthcoming book: "Signature Energy: The Vibrations of You." She blogs about writing, editing, and provides publishing wisdom on her website www.thepublishingauthority.com.

Other authors who have critiqued my work include:

Karla von Huben, author of several books, her recent book "The Youngest Elf and Other Stories: Further Adventures."

Lelia Rose Foreman, author of "Tales of Talifar."

Kumiko Olson, author of "From Tokyo To America: Seven Times Down Eight Times Up."

Jon Drury, author of "Lord, I Feel So Small."

I have received great advice from Andi Crockford who is writing about her world travels, James Chesky who writes about dragons, Amanda Cherry, Erika Work Jesse McClure, and Adam Stewart–short story expert.

I want to thank the *Coffee House Writers Group,* Portland OR with co-founders Elizabyth (Burtis) Harrington, and Mark Harrington. Elizabyth is the author of "Demonology: Book of Gabriel." Vargus Pike, poet, his most recent collection is: "July Song." Heather Self, author of "Backbeat."

Catherine Adee is writing a book I can't wait for her to publish. And more authors than I can list here.

Most importantly, I want to thank my editor, friend, and fellow puppy parent, Susan Frager. She continues to support me on my journey as an author, much to the consternation of her two spoiled beagles, Sophie and Spencer.

About the Author

Ilana Lehmann is like no one you have met before. A high school dropout, who went on to earn a Ph.D. She was born and raised in San Diego, CA and has lived at over 50 addresses across the United States including 6 years living in New England.

A former member of the Air Force Reserves and AFROTC student at San Diego State University, she chose to have a family rather than pursue her childhood dream to become an aerospace engineer, test pilot, and astronaut. Among her various careers, she has worked as a waitress, retail clerk, receptionist, psychotherapist, case manager, and rehabilitation counselor, before she decided to become a professor.

She has a bachelor's degree in psychology and a master's degree in guidance and counseling with an emphasis on community mental health. She earned her doctorate in Rehabilitation Counseling from Southern Illinois University. She is a Certified Rehabilitation Counselor, and previously was a National Board Certified Counselor. In 2009, she won an outstanding research award from the American Rehabilitation Counseling Association for her publication on the unintended consequences of the Family and Medical Leave Act.

Currently, she teaches research methods to masters and doctoral students for an online university. She is writing more books and promises to continue to write until she is no longer educational or entertaining. Dr. Lehmann is bossed around by Hobbes, her cat, and Susie Derkins, her Pembroke Welsh Corgi.

www.ingramcontent.com/pod-product-compliance
Lightning Source LLC
Chambersburg PA
CBHW070527010526
44110CB00050B/2174